FASHION-PLUS KNITS

You'll feel like a queen in these eight magnificent sweaters made with Homespun® by Lion Brand® Yarn Company. Homespun® is so-soft to the touch and features a large selection of gorgeous color blends. This bulky weight yarn works up in no time, and its rich texture allows you to create intriguing designs without complicated stitch patterns.

Homespun® is a bulky-weight, richly textured 98% acrylic-2% polyester blend, Homespun is machine washable and dryable. It weighs 6 oz (170 grams) per skein and has a length of 185 yds (167 meters). For the knitting gauge, 14 stitches and 20 rows should equal 4" (10 cm) on size 10 (6 mm) needles. For the crochet gauge, 10 single crochet and 10 rows should equal 4" (10 cm) on a size K-10.5 (6.5 mm) hook.

Production Team: Editorial Director, Lion Brand - Nancy Thomas; Editorial Writer - Kimber Ross; Graphic Artist - Rebecca J. Hester; and Photo Stylists - Karen Hall and Cassie Newsome.

We have made every effort to ensure that these instructions are accurate and complete. We cannot, however, be responsible for human error, typographical mistakes, or variations in individual work.

©2014 by Leisure Arts, Inc., 104 Champs Blvd. STE 100, Maumelle, AR 72113-6738. All rights reserved. This publication is protected under federal copyright laws. Reproduction or distribution of this publication or any other Leisure Arts publication, including publications which are out of print, is prohibited unless specifically authorized. This includes, but is not limited to, any form of reproduction or distribution on or through the Internet, including posting, scanning, or e-mail transmission.

GENERAL INSTRUCTIONS

ABBREVIATIONS

beg	begin(ning)
CC	Contrasting Color
cm	centimeters
dec	decreas(e)(s)(ing)
inc	increas(e)(s)(ing)
k	knit
MC	Main Color
p	purl
psso	pass slipped stitch over
rem	remain(s)(ing)
rep	repeat(s)(ing)
RS	right side
sc	single crochet
st(s)	stitch(es)
St st	Stockinette Stitch
tbl	through back loop(s)
tog	together
wyif	with yarn in front
WS	wrong side
yo	yarn over

* — When you see an asterisk used within a pattern row, the symbol indicates that later you will be told to repeat a portion of the instruction. Most often the instructions will say, repeat from * so many times.

** or *** — Used to set off a block of text. Look for a direction such as: repeat between **'s or ***'s so many times.

( ) or [ ] — Set off a short number of stitches that are repeated a series of times. For example: [2 sc, 2 dc, 2 sc in next stitch] twice.

GAUGE

Never underestimate the importance of gauge. Achieving the correct gauge assures that the finished size of your piece matches the finished size given in the pattern.

CHECKING YOUR GAUGE

Work a swatch that is at least 4″ (10 cm) square. Use the suggested needle size and the number of stitches given. For example, the standard LION BRAND® Homespun® gauge is: 14 sts + 20 rows = 4″ (10 cm) on size 10 (6 mm) needles. If your swatch is larger than 4″, you need to work it again using smaller needles; if it is smaller than 4″, try it with larger needles. This might require a swatch or two to get the exact gauge given in the pattern.

METRICS

As a handy reference, keep in mind that 1 ounce = approximately 28 grams and 1″ = 2.5 centimeters.

TERMS

continue in this way or as established — Once a pattern is set up (established), the instructions may tell you to continue in the same way.

fasten off — To end your piece, you need to simply pull the yarn through the last loop left on the hook. This keeps the last stitch intact and prevents the work from unraveling.

right side — Refers to the front of the piece.

work even — This is used to indicate an area worked as established without increasing or decreasing.

wrong side — Refers to the back of the piece.

MARKERS

As a convenience to you, we have used markers to help distinguish the beginning of a pattern. Place markers as instructed. You may use purchased markers or tie a length of contrasting color yarn around the needle. When you reach a marker on each row, slip it from the left needle to the right needle; remove it when no longer needed.

KNIT TERMINOLOGY	
UNITED STATES	INTERNATIONAL
gauge = tension	
bind off = cast off	
yarn over (yo) = yarn forward (yfwd) **or**	
yarn around needle (yrn)	

KNITTING NEEDLES	
UNITED STATES	METRIC (mm)
0	2
1	2.25
2	2.75
3	3.25
4	3.5
5	3.75
6	4
7	4.5
8	5
9	5.5
10	6
10½	6.5
11	8
13	9
15	10
17	12.75

■□□□ BEGINNER	Projects for first-time crocheters using basic stitches. Minimal shaping.
■■□□ EASY	Projects using yarn with basic stitches, repetitive stitch patterns, simple color changes, and simple shaping and finishing.
■■■□ INTERMEDIATE	Projects using a variety of techniques, such as basic lace patterns or color patterns, mid-level shaping and finishing.
■■■■ EXPERIENCED	Projects with intricate stitch patterns, techniques and dimension, such as non-repeating patterns, multi-color techniques, fine threads, small hooks, detailed shaping and refined finishing.

Yarn Weight Symbol & Names	SUPER FINE 1	FINE 2	LIGHT 3	MEDIUM 4	BULKY 5	SUPER BULKY 6
Type of Yarns in Category	Sock, Fingering, Baby	Sport, Baby	DK, Light Worsted	Worsted, Afghan, Aran	Chunky, Craft, Rug	Bulky, Roving

BASIC CROCHET STITCHES

■ ■ ■ ■ ■ ■ ■ ■ ■ ■ ■ ■ ■ ■ ■

■ SINGLE CROCHET

Insert hook in stitch indicated, yo and pull up a loop, yo and draw through both loops on hook **(Fig. 1) (abbreviated sc)**.

Fig. 1

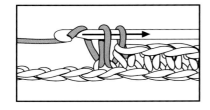

■ ZEROS

To consolidate the length of an involved pattern, Zeros are sometimes used so that all sizes can be combined. For example, increase every sixth row 5{1-0} time(s) means the first size would increase 5 times, the second size would increase once, and the largest size would do nothing.

BASIC KNIT STITCHES

■ STOCKINETTE STITCH

Knit one row or number of stitches indicated (right side), purl one row or number of stitches indicated. The knit side is smooth and flat *(Fig. 2a)*, and the purl side is bumpy *(Fig. 2b)*.

Fig. 2a   **Fig. 2b**

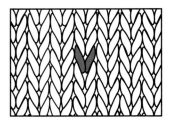 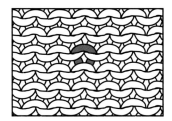

■ GARTER STITCH

Knit every row. Two rows of knitting make one horizontal ridge in your fabric *(Fig. 3)*.

Fig. 3

■ KNIT INCREASE

Knit the next stitch but do **not** slip the old stitch off the left needle *(Fig.Á4a)*. Insert the right needle into the **back** loop of the **same** stitch and knit it *(Fig.Á4b)*, then slip the old stitch off the left needle.

Fig. 4a   **Fig. 4b**

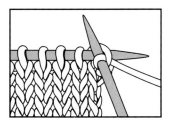 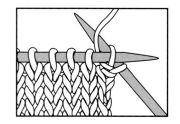

■ KNIT 2 TOGETHER
(abbreviated k2 tog)

Insert the right needle into the **front** of the first two stitches on the left needle as if to **knit** *(Fig. 5)*, then **knit** them together as if they were one stitch.

Fig. 5

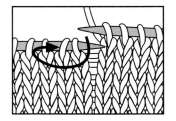

■ SLIP, SLIP, KNIT
(abbreviated ssk)

(With yarn in back of work,) separately slip two stitches as if to **knit** *(Fig. 6a)*. Insert the left needle into the **front** of both slipped stitches *(Fig. 6b)* and knit them together *(Fig. 6c)*.

Fig. 6a   **Fig. 6b**

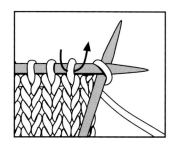 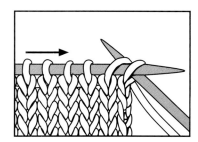

Fig. 6c

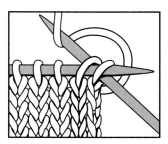

▪ SLIP 1, KNIT 1, PASS SLIPPED STITCH OVER
(abbreviated slip 1, k1, psso)
Slip one stitch as if to **knit**. Knit the next stitch. With the left needle, bring the slipped stitch over the knit stitch *(Fig. 7)* and off the needle.

Fig. 7

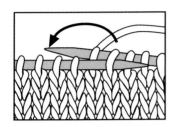

▪ SLIP 2 TOG, KNIT 1, PASS 2 SLIPPED STITCHES OVER
(abbreviated slip 2 tog, slip, k1, p2sso)
With yarn in back, separately slip two stitches as if to **knit2tog** *(Fig. 8a)*, then knit the next stitch. With the left needle, bring both slipped stitches over the knit stitch *(Fig. 8b)* and off the needle.

Fig. 8a

Fig. 8b

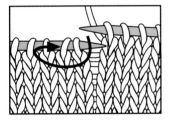 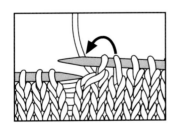

▪ SLIP 1, KNIT 2 TOGETHER, PASS SLIPPED STITCH OVER
(abbreviated slip 1, k2tog, psso)
Slip one stitch as if to **knit** *(Fig. 9a)*, then knit the next two stitches together. With the left needle, bring the slipped stitch over the stitch just made *(Fig. 9b)* and off the needle.

Fig. 9a **Fig. 9b**

 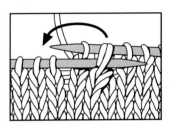

▪ YARN OVER *(abbreviated yo)*
After a knit stitch, before a knit stitch
Bring the yarn forward **between** the needles, then back **over** the top of the right hand needle, so that it is now in position to knit the next stitch *(Fig. 10)*.

Fig. 10

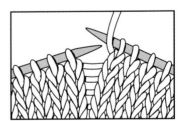

5

MIDNIGHT EXPRESS VEST

Designed by Susan Esser

SIZE
One size
Finished Chest Measurement: 50" (127 cm)
Finished Length: 28" (71 cm)
(including front points)

⬛⬛⬛◻ **INTERMEDIATE**

MATERIALS

- ⬛ LION BRAND® Homespun® #319 Adirondack - 4 skeins or color of your choice
- ⬛ Knitting needles size 10 (6 mm) or size needed for gauge
- ⬛ Double-pointed knitting needles size 8 (5 mm)

GAUGE: 12 sts and 24 rows = 4" (10 cm) in Garter st (knit every row) on larger needles

NOTES
1. Vest is knitted side-to-side.
2. ALL increases and decreases are made at the BEGINNING of a row.
3. Use your favorite methods of increase and decrease. The ones used in the sample are increase: (K 1 (edge stitch), backward loop) and decrease: (K 1 (edge stitch), k2tog tbl) respectively.
4. Mark the RS with a safety pin, also use a marker to designate the top or bottom of the vest.
5. Some width may be added by knitting extra rows in sections D and H (make sure you add the same number of rows to BOTH sections). Yarn quantities may need to be adjusted.

STITCH GUIDE

Knitted-on method of cast on: With slip knot or stitch on left needle, * insert right needle into st and k, do not drop st from left needle, slip just made st tbl onto left needle; rep from *.

VEST

Cast on 36 sts.

SECTION A

Inc 1 st at beg of row every row until piece measures 5" from beg. 66 sts/Row 30.

SECTION B

RS: Dec 1 st at beg of row, k across.

WS: Inc 1 st at beg of row, k across.

Rep last 2 rows until piece measures 6¹/₂" from beg. 66 sts/Row 38.

RS Row: Dec 1 st at beg of row, k across; cast on 14 sts. 79 sts/Row 39.

SECTION C

WS: Knit across.

RS: Dec 1 st at beg of row, knit across.

Rep last 2 rows until piece measures 10" from beg. 69 sts/Row 59.

WS Row: Bind off 33 sts, knit across. 36 sts/Row 60.

SECTION D

Work even on 36 sts until piece measures 16" from beg. 36 sts/Row 96.

RS Row: Knit across; cast on 33 sts. 69 sts/Row 97.

SECTION E

Work even on 69 sts until piece measures 19¹/₂" from beg. 69 sts/Row 117.

WS Row: Bind off 14 sts, knit across. 55 sts/Row 118.

SECTION F

Work even on 55 sts until piece measures 30¹/₂" from beg. 55 sts/Row 182.

RS Row: Knit across; cast on 14 sts – 69 sts/Row 183.

SECTION G

Work even on 69 sts until piece measures 34" from beg. 69 sts/Row 203.

WS Row: Bind off 33 sts; knit across. 36 sts/Row 204.

SECTION H

Work even on 36 sts until piece measures 40" from beg. 36 sts/Row 240.

RS Row: Knit across; cast on 33 sts. 69 sts/Row 241.

SECTION I

WS: Knit across.

RS: Inc 1 st at beg of row, knit across.

Rep last 2 rows until piece measures 43¹/₂" from beg. 79 sts/Row 261.

WS Row: Bind off 13 sts, knit across. 66 sts/Row 262.

SECTION J

RS: Inc 1 st at beg of row, knit across.

WS: Dec 1 st at beg of row, knit across.

Rep last 2 rows until piece measures 45" from beg. 66 sts/Row 270.

SECTION K

RS: Dec 1 st at beg of row, knit across.

WS: Dec 1 st at beg of row, knit across.

Rep last 2 rows until piece measures 50" from beg. 36 sts/Row 300.

Bind off all sts

(**Note:** Do not fasten off last st if you plan on working CurlyQ Edging).

FINISHING

Sew shoulder seams invisibly.

EDGINGS

Here are two different edgings (these are for looks and also stability):

APPLIED I-CORD EDGING

This is to be applied on the RS after the Vest is completed. Begin by casting on 3 sts using double-pointed needles.

Work every row as follows: Knit 2 sts, slip 1 as if to knit, yo, then insert needle into the Vest edge and draw up a loop, knitting a stitch – 5 sts on right needle. Insert left needle into both the yo and the slipped st and lift them over the last stitch (binding off 2 sts). This is a little tight, but it will get easier as you go. Now slide sts to other end of the needle and begin again without turning your work. Work extra rows of I-cord when going around corners to prevent puckering.

CURLYQ EDGING

When you finish binding off the last row on the Vest, you'll have 1 st left. Put it on your left needle, then continue with:

* Cast on 2 sts using "knitted-on" method, then bind off 4 sts (inserting needle into the sweater edge and drawing up a loop to create the additional sts needed); rep around the entire vest, including armholes.

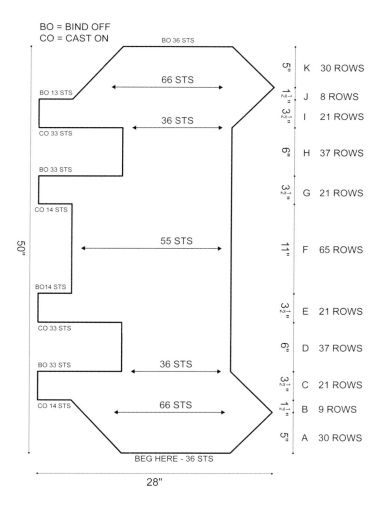

BO = BIND OFF
CO = CAST ON

BO 36 STS

BO 13 STS

CO 33 STS

BO 33 STS

CO 14 STS

BO14 STS

CO 33 STS

BO 33 STS

CO 14 STS

66 STS

36 STS

55 STS

36 STS

66 STS

50"

28"

BEG HERE - 36 STS

5"	K	30 ROWS
1½"	J	8 ROWS
3½"	I	21 ROWS
6"	H	37 ROWS
3½"	G	21 ROWS
11"	F	65 ROWS
3½"	E	21 ROWS
6"	D	37 ROWS
3½"	C	21 ROWS
1½"	B	9 ROWS
5"	A	30 ROWS

MITERED SQUARES VEST

Designed by Susan Esser

SIZE
Finished Chest Measurement
L	42″	(106.75 cm)
1X	46″	(116.75 cm)
2X	50″	(127 cm)
3X	56″	(142.25 cm)
4X	60″	(152.5 cm)

Finished Length
L	24″	(61 cm)
1X	25$\frac{1}{2}$″	(64.75 cm)
2X	27″	(68.5 cm)
3X	27″	(68.5 cm)
4X	28$\frac{1}{2}$″	(72.25 cm)

◖■■■▭ INTERMEDIATE

Size Note: Instructions are written for Large size, with sizes 1X, 2X, 3X, and 4X in braces [ ]. Instructions will be easier to read if you circle all the numbers pertaining to your size. If only one number is given, it applies to all sizes.

MATERIALS
BULKY 5

■ LION BRAND® Homespun®
   #320 Regency - 2 [3, 3, 3, 4] skeins (A)
   #341 Windsor - 2 [3, 3, 3, 3] skeins (B)
   or colors of your choice
■ Knitting needles size 10 (6 mm) or size needed for gauge
■ Double-pointed needles size 8 (5 mm)
■ Large-eyed, blunt needle

GAUGE: 12 sts and 24 rows = 4″ (10 cm) in Garter st (k every row).

STITCH GUIDE
Double Decrease (DD) Slip 2 sts as if to k2tog, k next st, pass 2 slipped sts over just made st. (**Note** Decreases are worked only on right side of work.)

Knitted-on method of cast on: With slip knot or stitch on left needle, * insert right needle into st and k, do not drop st from left needle, slip just made st tbl onto left needle; rep from *.

NOTES
1. For Custom Fit
Decide on **shoulder** width you desire. For example: 16" from shoulder to shoulder equals 16" for the Back, and 16" for the Front, which combined equals 32". Now measure the desired **chest** width, plus some extra for ease. For a finished Vest to measure 40", then subtract 32" (the total of the Front and Back squares) from that chest measurement to get the number of inches needed for side panels; in this case: 40 − 32 = 8, so <u>each</u> side panel (under each arm) should be 4". If you're lucky enough to need side panels the same width as one of your mitered squares, then just knit 8 more squares and attach these as your side panels.
2. For smooth edges which allow for picking up the sts neatly later: ON EVERY ROW, knit the first st through the back loop, and slip the last st purlwise with yarn in front (wyif).
3. Alternate colors by changing at the end of each square.

SQUARE 1
Cast on 23 [25, 27, 27, 29] sts with A or B (refer to schematic).

Row 1 (RS): K 10 [11, 12, 12, 13], DD, k 10 [11, 12, 12, 13]; mark RS of work.

Row 2 (WS): K 10 [11, 12, 12, 13], slip 1 wyif, k 10 [11, 12, 12, 13].

Row 3: K 9 [10, 11, 11, 12], DD, k 9 [10, 11, 11, 12].

Row 4: K 9 [10, 11, 11, 12], slip 1 wyif, k 9 [10, 11, 11, 12].

Continue dec in this way, working 1 less st before and after DD on RS (slip 1 on WS) until 5 sts rem.

Next Row (RS): K 1, DD, k 1.

Last Row: DD, bind off last st.

SQUARE 2 for the Left Front
Following the schematic in this pattern, with RS facing, pick up 12 [13, 14, 14, 15] sts down the left edge of the square you have just finished. Into that last st you have just picked up, begin casting on 11 [12, 13, 13, 14] more sts. 23 [25, 27, 27, 29] sts.

Complete as for Square 1.

SQUARE 3 for the Left Front
With RS facing, cast on 11 [12, 13, 13, 14] sts, then pick up 12 [13, 14, 14, 15] sts across the top edge of Square 1. 23 [25, 27, 27, 29] sts.

Complete as for Square 1.

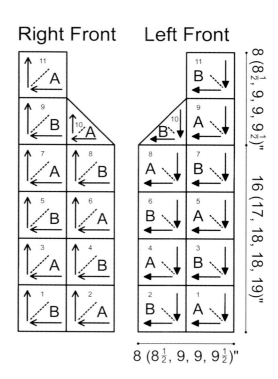

8 (8½, 9, 9, 9½)"

SQUARE 4 for the Left Front

With RS facing, pick up 11 [12, 13, 13, 14] sts down the left side of the square you have just finished, pick up 1 st in the corner, pick up 11 [12, 13, 13, 14] sts across the top of Square 2. 23 [25, 27, 27, 29] sts.

Complete as for Square 1.

Continue following the squares numerically on the chart, casting on and picking up sts as called for in the direction of the arrows.

HALF SQUARE 10 (both Fronts)

Pick up 11 [12, 13, 13, 14] sts along the side or top of the square, pick up 1 st in the corner, pick up 11 [12, 13, 13, 14] sts across the top or side of the other square. 23 [25, 27, 27, 29] sts.

Continue as for Square 1, and AT SAME TIME, k2tog at the beg of every row.

Sizes L, 2X, 3X: When 3 sts rem, DD and bind off.

Sizes 1X and 4X: When 5 sts rem, finish off as for last two rows of Square 1.

RIGHT FRONT AND BACK

Work as for Left Front beginning with Square 1, following schematics for placement and color.

SIDE PANELS

With RS facing, pick up and k 46 [48, 51, 51, 54] sts evenly along side edges of lower 4 squares on each Front.

Work 5 [6, 7, 10, 11]" in Garter st. Bind off.

A good-looking variation: Dec 1 stitch at the beg of every row for 2½ [3, 3½, 5, 5½]", then increase 1 stitch at the beg of every row for 2½ [3, 3½, 5, 5½]" more until side panel measures 5 [6, 7, 10, 11]" from beg. Bind off.

FINISHING

Sew Front Side Panels invisibly to lower 4 squares on each side of Back. Sew shoulders together.

The last finishing touch is to work Applied I-Cord around entire edges (including armholes.):

APPLIED I CORD

This is to be applied on the right side after the Vest is completely knitted and assembled.

Using 2 double-pointed needles, cast on 3 sts.

Now work every row as follows: Knit 2 sts, slip 1 as if to knit, yo, then insert right needle into the Vest edge and knit a stitch. 5 sts on right needle. Insert left needle into both the yo and the slipped stitch and lift them over the last stitch (binding off 2 sts). This is a little tight, but it will get easier the more you do it. Without turning work, slide sts to other end of needle and begin again, working around all edges. Work extra I-cord stitches when going around corners to prevent puckering.

Back

Side Panels

16 (17, 18, 18, 19)"

24 (25½, 27, 27, 28½)"

16 (17, 18, 18, 19)"

5 (6, 7, 10, 11)"

Bess' V-Neck Lace Pullover

Designed by Kathleen Power Johnson

SIZES
Finished Chest

L	48" (121.5 cm)
1X	53" (134 cm)
2X	56" (142.25 cm)
3X	64" (162.5 cm)
4X	69" (175 cm)

■■◻◻▷ EASY

Size Note: Instructions are written for Large size, with sizes 1X, 2X, 3X, and 4X in braces [ ]. Instructions will be easier to read if you circle all the numbers pertaining to your size. If only one number is given, it applies to all sizes.

MATERIALS

BULKY 5

- LION BRAND® Homespun® #362 Quartz - 4 [5, 5, 6, 6] skeins or color of your choice
- Knitting needles size 10½ (6.5 mm) or size needed for gauge
- Size 10½ (6.5 mm) circular needle, 16" long
- 1 ring marker
- Large-eyed, blunt needle

GAUGE: 12 sts and 21 rows = 4" (10 cm) in St st (k on RS, p on WS).

STITCH GUIDE

ssk (slip, slip, knit) Slip next 2 sts as if to knit, one at a time, to right needle; insert left needle into fronts of these 2 sts and k them tog.

PATTERN STITCH

Diagonal Openwork (4 sts + 2 + 2 selvage sts)
Row 1 (WS) and all odd-numbered rows: Purl.
Row 2: K 1, * k 1, yo, slip 1-k2tog-psso, yo; rep from * to last 3 sts, k 3.
Row 4: K 3, * yo, slip 1-k2tog-psso, yo, k 1; rep from * to last st, k 1.
Row 6: K 1, k2tog, yo, k 1, yo, * slip 1-k2tog-psso, yo, k1, yo; rep from * to last 4 sts, slip 1-k 1-psso, k 2.
Row 8: K 2, k2tog, yo, k 1, yo; * slip 1-k2tog-psso, yo, k1, yo; rep from * to last 3 sts, slip 1-k 1-psso, k 1.
Repeat Rows 1 - 8 for Pattern.

BACK

Cast on 72 [80, 84, 96, 104] sts. Work in Pattern St for 4″ from beg, ending with Row 1.

Continue in St st until Back measures 19³/₄ [20, 20, 20, 20]″ from beg, or desired length to underarm.

Shape Armhole: Bind off 5 [5, 7, 7, 7] sts at beg of next 2 rows, then 2 sts at the beg of the following 2 [2, 2, 4, 4] rows.

Dec 1 st each end of every other row 3 [6, 6, 9, 12] times.

Work even on 52 [54, 54, 56, 58] sts until Armhole measures 7¹/₄ [7¹/₂, 8, 8¹/₂, 9]″.

Shape Shoulders: Bind off 4 [5, 5, 5, 6] sts at the beg of the next 2 rows, 4 [4, 4, 5, 5] sts at the beg of the next 2 rows and 4 sts at the beg of the last 2 rows. Loosely bind off remaining 28 neck sts.

FRONT

Work as for Back, placing a marker after the 36th [40th, 42nd, 48th, 52nd] st before beg armhole shaping.

When the center Front measures 19 [19¹/₂, 20, 20¹/₂, 21]″ from beg, **Shape Neckline:** Work across to within 2 sts of marker, k2tog; join a separate skein of yarn, ssk, and complete row.

Working both sides at the same time, dec 1 st at each neck edge [every 2nd row, then every 4th row] 4 times (dec 8 sts each side), then every 2nd row 5 times. AT SAME TIME, when side measures 19³/₄ [20, 20, 20, 20]″ from beg, **Shape Armhole** as for Back.

Work even until Front measures the same as Back to shoulders, shape as for Back.

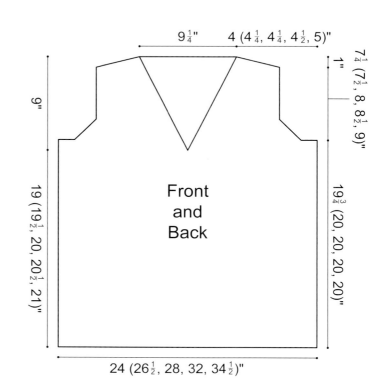

9¹/₄″   4 (4¹/₄, 4¹/₄, 4¹/₂, 5)″

7¹/₄ (7¹/₂, 8, 8¹/₂, 9)″

1″

9″

19 (19¹/₂, 20, 20¹/₂, 21)″

Front and Back

19³/₄ (20, 20, 20, 20)″

24 (26¹/₂, 28, 32, 34¹/₂)″

SLEEVES – Make 2

Cast on 40 sts and work in Pattern st for 2",
ending with Row 1.

Continue in St st, inc 1 st each end of every 10th
row 2 [0, 0, 0, 0] times, every 8th row 5 [7, 1, 0,
0] times, every 6th row 0 [1, 9, 7, 7] times and
every 4th row 0 [0, 0, 5, 5] times.

Work even on 54 [56, 60, 64, 64] sts until Sleeve
measures 14¾ [15¼, 15, 15½, 15¼]" from beg,
or desired length to underarm.

Cap Shaping: Bind off 5 [5, 7, 7, 7] sts at beg of
next 2 rows, then 2 sts at the beg of the following
2 [2, 2, 4, 4] rows.

Dec 1 st each end of every other row 7 [8, 8, 8,
8] times. 26 sts.

When cap measures 5¾ [6, 6½, 7, 7½]" from
initial bind off, bind off 3 sts at the beg of the next
4 rows. Loosely bind off remaining 14 sts.

FINISHING

Sew shoulder seams.

NECKBAND

With right side facing, circle needle and beginning
at center front, pick up 26 sts along right front
neck, 24 sts across back neck, and 26 sts along
left front neck.

Work Pattern st on 76 sts without joining until
Band measures 1¼", ending with Row 6. Bind off
in knit.

Sew band in place, lapping right side over left
side

Sew Sleeves into armholes, then sew side and
Sleeve seams.

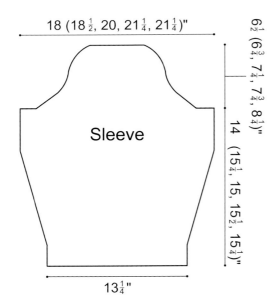

18 (18½, 20, 21¼, 21¼)"

6½ (6¾, 7¼, 7¾, 8¼)"

14 (15¼, 15, 15½, 15¼)"

Sleeve

13¼"

KYOKI'S KIMONO

Designed by Kathleen Power Johnson

SIZES
Finished Chest Measurement

L	55"	(139.75 cm)
1X	58"	(147.25 cm)
2X	62"	(157.5 cm)
3X	67"	(170 cm)
4X	71"	(180.25 cm)

■■□□ **EASY**

Size Note: Instructions are written for Large size, with sizes 1X, 2X, 3X, and 4X in braces [ ]. Instructions will be easier to read if you circle all the numbers pertaining to your size. If only one number is given, it applies to all sizes.

MATERIALS
- LION BRAND® Homespun® **BULKY 5**
  - #321 Williamsburg (MC) - 5 [5, 6, 7, 8] skeins
  - #302 Colonial (CC) - 1 skein
    or colors of your choice
- Knitting needles size 10½ (6.5 mm) or size needed for gauge
- Crochet hook size K-10½ (6.5 mm)
- 4 stitch holders
- Large-eyed, blunt needle

GAUGE: 12 sts and 21 rows = 4" (10 cm) in St st (k on RS, p on WS).

STITCH GUIDE

3-Needle Bind Off With RS together, hold in one hand 2 needles with equal number of sts on each. With third needle, knit tog one st from each needle, * knit tog one st from each needle, pass first st worked over second to bind off, rep from * across to last st. Cut working yarn and pull through last st to secure.

BACK

With MC, cast on 84 [89, 95, 103, 109] sts.

Work even in St st until piece measures 19¼" from beg.

Shape Armhole: Bind off 8 [8, 10, 10, 10] sts at beg of next 2 rows, and 2 sts at the beg of the next 4 [4, 4, 6, 6] rows. Dec 1 st each end every other row 5 [6, 6, 8, 11] times.

Work even on 50 [53, 55, 55, 55] sts until Back measures 29 [29¼, 29½, 30, 30¼]" from beg.

Shape Neck: Work across 18 [19, 19, 19, 19] sts, bind off 14 [15, 17, 17, 17] sts, complete row. Working with a separate ball of yarn for each side, work one row even, then bind off 2 sts at each neck edge. Place 16 [17, 17, 17, 17] sts for each shoulder on stitch holders.

LEFT FRONT

With MC cast on 33 [35, 37, 41, 44] sts, and with CC, cast on 9 [10, 11, 11, 11] sts, (making sure to cross yarns when changing colors) 42 [45, 48, 52, 55] sts.

Working MC sts in St st and CC band sts in Garter st (k every row), maintain pattern, crossing yarns when changing color, working until piece measures same as Back to armhole.

Shape Armhole as for Back.

Work even on 25 [27, 28, 28, 28] sts until piece measures 30 [30¼, 30½, 31, 31¼]" from beg.

Place 16 [17, 17, 17, 17] shoulder sts and 9 [10, 11, 11, 11] band sts on holder.

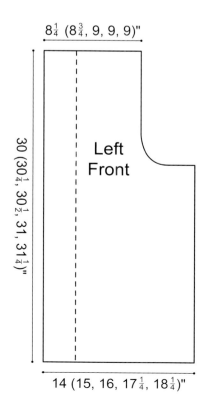

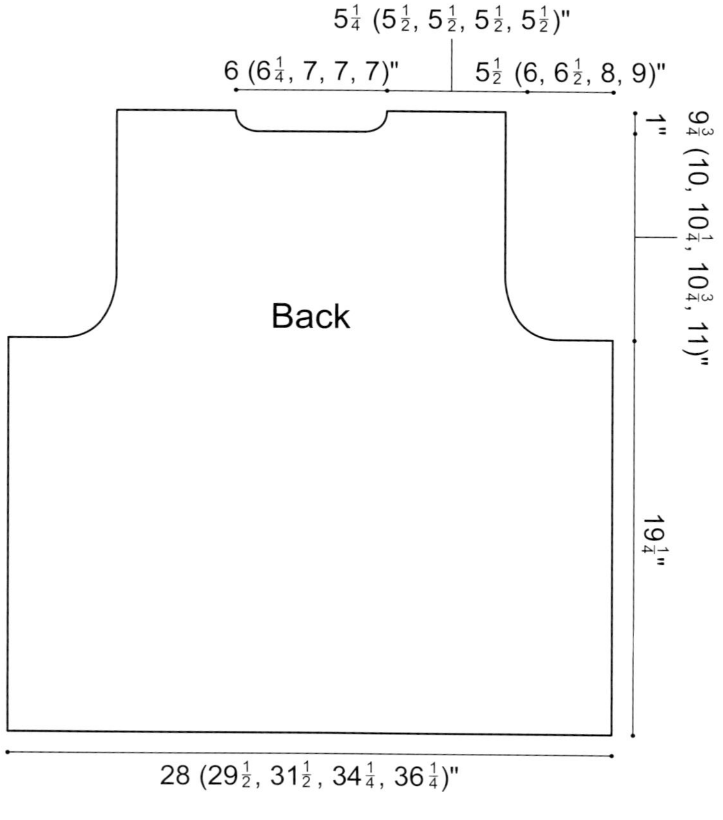

5¼ (5½, 5½, 5½, 5½)"

6 (6¼, 7, 7, 7)" 5½ (6, 6½, 8, 9)"

1"

9¾ (10, 10¼, 10¾, 11)"

Back

19¼"

28 (29½, 31½, 34¼, 36¼)"

8¼ (8¾, 9, 9, 9)"

30 (30¼, 30½, 31, 31¼)"

Left Front

14 (15, 16, 17¼, 18¼)"

RIGHT FRONT

With CC, cast on 9 [10, 11, 11, 11] sts, and with MC, cast on 33 [35, 37, 41, 44] sts, making sure to cross yarns when changing colors.

Work as for Left Front, reversing shaping.

SLEEVES – Make 2

With CC cast on 41 sts.

Work in Garter st for 3″. AT SAME TIME, inc each end of every 4th row 13 [14, 11, 12, 10] times; every other row 0 [0, 5, 5, 8] times; and changing to MC and St st when Sleeve measures 3″ from cast on row.

Work even on 67 [69, 73, 75, 77] sts until Sleeve measures 13¼ [13¾, 13¾, 14¼, 14¼]″ from beg or desired length to underarm.

Sleeve Cap Shaping: Bind off 8 [8, 10, 10, 10] sts at beg of next 2 rows, and 2 sts at the beg of the next 4 [4, 4, 6, 6] rows. Dec 1 st each end of every other row 7 [9, 7, 3, 4] times, and every 4th row 4 [3, 4, 6, 6] times. Bind off 2 sts at the beg of the next 4 rows. Bind off remaining 13 [13, 15, 17, 17] sts.

FINISHING

Remove 16 [17, 17, 17, 17] shoulder sts from holders and knit shoulder seams tog with 3-needle bind off.

Sew Sleeves to armholes, then Sleeve and side seams.

With crochet hook, work 1 row sc around entire lower edge using CC for edge of front bands and MC for the body of the Jacket.

Neckband: Mark center Back.

For each side: place 9 [10, 11, 11, 11] band sts on needle. Work in Garter st as established until free portion of band reaches the center back.

Sew band in place around back neck from the underside so it doesn't show when band is folded to the outside of Jacket neck.

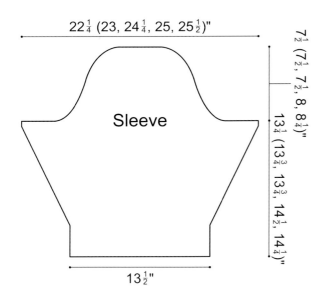

22¼ (23, 24¼, 25, 25½)″

Sleeve

7½ (7½, 7½, 8, 8¼)″

13¼ (13¾, 13¾, 14½, 14¼)″

13½″

BONITA'S RIBBED COAT

Designed by Kathleen Power Johnson

SIZES
Finished Chest

L	54" (137 cm)
1X	58" (147 cm)
2X	62" (157 cm)
3X	66" (167 cm)
4X	72" (183 cm)

 **EASY +**

Size Note: Instructions are written for Large size, with sizes 1X, 2X, 3X, and 4X in braces [ ]. Instructions will be easier to read if you circle all the numbers pertaining to your size. If only one number is given, it applies to all sizes.

MATERIALS
- LION BRAND® Homespun® **BULKY 5**
  #343 Romanesque - 8 [8, 9, 10, 11] skeins or color of your choice
- Knitting needles sizes 8 (5 mm), 10½ (6.5 mm), and 11 (8 mm) or size needed for gauge
- 2 stitch holders
- Nine ⅝" (15.75 mm) buttons (JHB International #1584 shown)
- Large-eyed, blunt needle

GAUGE: 15 sts and 21 rows = 4" (10 cm) in Pattern stitch on size 10½ needles (measured without stretching).

PATTERN STITCH
"Mistake" Rib (multiple of 4 sts + 3)
Row 1: * K 2, p 2; repeat from *, ending k 2, p 1. Repeat Row 1 for pattern.

NOTE
Because of the tendency of this pattern stitch to shorten the fabric as it's laid out for measuring, row counts for all vertical measurements are included.

STITCH GUIDE
ssk (slip, slip, knit) Slip next 2 sts as if to knit, one at a time, to right needle; insert left needle into fronts of these 2 sts and k them together.

BACK
With largest needles, cast on 99 [107, 115, 123, 135] sts.

Marking RS row, change to middle size needles and work in Pattern st until piece measures 12" (64 rows) from beg, ending with a WS row.

Next Row: Place marker and inc 1 st at beg and end of row - *selvage sts.* 101 [109, 117, 125, 137] sts.

Continue even in Pattern, slipping first st of each row as if to purl, until Back measures 23½ [24, 24, 24¾, 25]" (123 [126, 126, 130, 131] rows) from beg.

Shape Armhole: Bind off 8 [8, 8, 10, 12] sts at beg of next 2 rows.

Dec 1 st each end of every 4th row 2 [0, 0, 0, 0] times, then every other row 25 [30, 33, 35, 38] times. Bind off remaining 31 [33, 35, 35, 37] sts for neckline.

LEFT FRONT
With largest needles, cast on 51 [55, 59, 63, 67] sts. Marking RS row, change to middle size needles and work in Pattern st until piece measures 12" (64 rows) from beg, ending with a WS row.

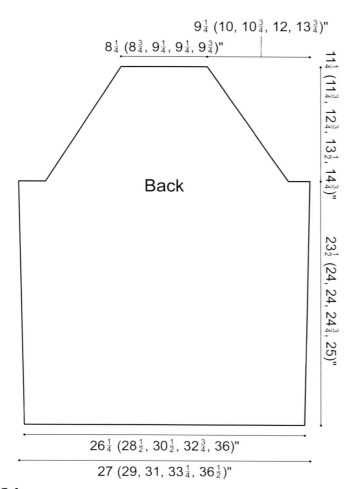

9¼ (10, 10¾, 12, 13¾)"

8¼ (8¾, 9¼, 9¼, 9¾)"

11¼ (11¾, 12¾, 13½, 14¾)"

23½ (24, 24, 24¾, 25)"

Back

26¼ (28½, 30½, 32¾, 36)"

27 (29, 31, 33¼, 36½)"

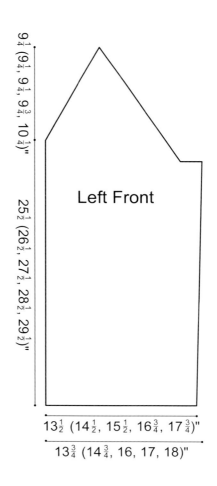

9¼ (9¼, 9¼, 9¾, 10¼)"

25½ (26½, 27½, 28½, 29½)"

Left Front

13½ (14½, 15½, 16¾, 17¾)"

13¾ (14¾, 16, 17, 18)"

Next Row: Place marker and inc 1 st at beg of row - *selvage st* . 52 [56, 60, 64, 68] sts.

Continue even in Pattern st, slipping first st of each RS row, until Left Front measures $23\frac{1}{2}$ [24, 24, $24\frac{3}{4}$, 25]"; (123 [126, 126, 130, 131] rows) from beg.

Shape Armhole as for Back. AT SAME TIME, when the center front edge measures $25\frac{1}{2}$ [$26\frac{1}{2}$, $27\frac{1}{2}$, $28\frac{1}{2}$, $29\frac{1}{2}$)"; [134 [140, 144, 150, 154] rows) from beg, **Shape Neckline:** Dec 1 st at end of every 4th RS row 7 [6, 5, 5, 6] times, then every other row 9 [11, 13, 13, 11] times, 1 st remains. Fasten off.

RIGHT FRONT
Work as for Left Front, reversing shaping and slipping the first st of every WS row above marker.

SLEEVES – Make 2
With largest needles, cast on 39 [39, 43, 43, 43] sts.

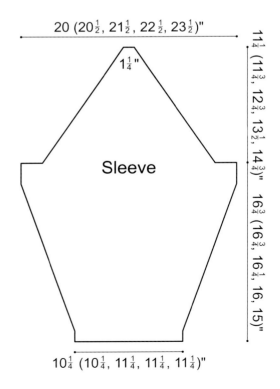

20 ($20\frac{1}{2}$, $21\frac{1}{2}$, $22\frac{1}{2}$, $23\frac{1}{2}$)"

$1\frac{1}{4}$"

Sleeve

$11\frac{1}{4}$ ($11\frac{3}{4}$, $12\frac{3}{4}$, $13\frac{1}{2}$, $14\frac{3}{4}$)"

$16\frac{3}{4}$ ($16\frac{3}{4}$, $16\frac{1}{4}$, 16, 15)"

$10\frac{1}{4}$ ($10\frac{1}{4}$, $11\frac{1}{4}$, $11\frac{1}{4}$, $11\frac{1}{4}$)"

Marking RS row, change to middle size needles and work in Pattern st, inc 1 st each end of every 6th row 5 [3, 2, 0, 0] times; every 4th row 13 [16, 17, 18, 14] times; and every other row 0 [0, 0, 3, 9] times.

Work even on 75 [77, 81, 85, 89] sts until Sleeve measures $16\frac{3}{4}$ ($16\frac{3}{4}$, $16\frac{1}{4}$, 16, 15)" from cast on row.

Shape Raglan Cap: Bind off 8 [8, 8, 10, 12] sts at beg of next 2 rows.

Dec 1 st each end of every 4th row 2 [2, 3, 5, 8] times and every other row 25 [26, 27, 25, 22] times. Place remaining 5 sts on holder.

FINISHING
Sew Sleeves to Back and two Fronts.

Sew Sleeve and side seams above markers.

Band: With smallest needles, cast on 5 sts.

With RS facing, knit up 1 st in edge of Right Front, just above first cast on st. * Turn. P 2, (k 1, p 1) twice. Turn. (K 1, p 1) twice, ssk, knit up 1 st in edge; repeat from * around entire front and neckline edges, placing first buttonhole 9 [10, 11, 12, 13]"; (45 [50, 55, 60, 65] rows) from beg and spacing remaining 8 buttonholes 2" (10 rows) apart.

Work buttonhole on RS row as follows: K 1, p 1, ssk, yarn over, ssk, knit up 1 st in edge. Turn. P 2, k 1 into yarn over, p 1, k 1, p 1. Turn.

Sew buttons in place on Left Front band to correspond to buttonholes.

Optional Belt: With middle size needles, cast on 7 sts.

Row 1: K 1, *p 1, k 1; repeat from * to end.

Row 2: P 1, *k 1, p 1; repeat from * to end.

Work in Rib for 72" or desired length and bind off.

FLATTERING WRAP

Designed by Kennita Tully

SIZE
Width: 48" (122 cm)
Length: 32" (81.25 cm)

■□□□ **BEGINNER**

MATERIALS
■ LION BRAND® Homespun® BULKY 5
  #338 Nouveau - 9 skeins
    or color of your choice
■ Knitting needle circular size 10 (6 mm) or size
    needed for gauge.
■ Large-eyed, blunt needle

GAUGE: 12 stitches and 22 rows = 4" (10 cm)
when hanging.

BACK
Cast on 144 stitches.

Work in Garter Stitch (knit every row) until piece
measures 31" from beginning.

Shape Shoulders: Bind off 21 stitches at beginning
of next 2 rows, then 20 stitches at beginning of
next 4 rows. Bind off remaining 22 stitches for
neck.

RIGHT FRONT
Cast on 72 stitches and work as for Back until
piece measures 30" from beginning.

Shape Neck: Decrease one stitch every row at
neck edge 11 times and at the same time shape
shoulders as for Back when Front measures same
as Back to shoulder.

LEFT FRONT
Work same as for Right Front, reversing shaping.

FINISHING
Seam shoulders.

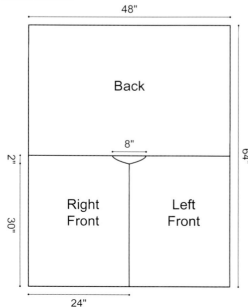

THE RICK SHAWL

Designed by Susan Esser

Finished Size:
80" (203.25 cm) across top edge x 39" (99 cm) from center to lower point

◼◼◼◻ INTERMEDIATE

MATERIALS

BULKY **5**

- ◼ LION BRAND® Homespun®
  #335 Prairie - 4 skeins
  #347 Mediterranean - 3 skeins
  or colors of your choice
- ◼ Knitting needles circular size 10½ (6.5 mm) 29" or longer or size needed for gauge
- ◼ Knitting needles at least 2 sizes larger than size used to knit Shawl
- ◼ Knitting needles size 9 (5.5 mm) for Rick Rack trim
- ◼ Safety pin
- ◼ Stitch marker

GAUGE: 13 sts and 26 rows = 4" (10 cm) in Garter st (k every row) on larger needles

STITCH GUIDE

Yo at beg of row Begin the row with the yarn in the front (instead of in the back as normal). As you knit your first stitch, bring the yarn over the needle. 2 stitches on the needle.

Inc 1 Increase 1 st by knitting into the front and back of a stitch.

K2tog tbl Knit the next 2 stitches together through the back loops.

Knitted-on method of cast on With slip knot or stitch on left needle, *insert right needle into st and k, do not drop st from left needle, slip just made st tbl onto left needle; rep from *.

NOTES
1. Place pin to indicate RS of work.
2. Change colors on RS rows whenever it pleases you, making varied width stripes throughout, saving one full skein for Edging.

SHAWL

Using circular needle, cast on 6 sts.

Row 1 (RS): K 3, place marker, k 3.

Row 2 (WS): Yo, k 3, slip marker (sm), k 3.

Row 3: Yo, k 2, inc 1, sm, k 1, inc 1, k 2.

Row 4: Yo, k 5, sm, k 5.

Row 5: Yo, k 4, inc 1, sm, k 1, inc 1, k 4.

Row 6: Yo, k 7, sm, k 7.

Row 7: Yo, k 6, inc 1, sm, k 1, inc 1, k 6.

Row 8: Yo, k 9, sm, k 9. 19 sts.

Row 9: Yo, k 6, k2tog, yo, inc 1, sm, k 1, inc 1, yo, k2tog tbl, k 6.

Row 10: Yo, k 11, sm, k 11.

Row 11: Yo, k 6, k2tog, yo, k 2, inc 1, sm, k 1, inc 1, k 2, yo, k2tog tbl, k 6.

Row 12: Yo, knit across all stitches.

Row 13: Yo, k 6, k2tog, yo; k to 1 st before marker, inc 1, sm, k 1, inc 1, k to last 8 sts; yo, k2tog tbl, k 6.

Row 14: Yo, knit across all stitches. 31 sts.

Rep Rows 13-14 until there are 359 sts or to desired size.

Bind off all stitches with a needle at least 2 sizes larger than the one you used to knit the Shawl.

RICK RACK EDGING

Edging is made separately and attached at points of rick rack to Shawl, running the yarn as invisibly as possible through edge of Shawl to get to next point to be tacked on. You may wish to use a thinner, smoother yarn or sewing thread in a matching color to attach rick rack trim.

Begin by casting on 8 sts using smaller needle.

* Work 9 rows in Garter st; bind off 4 sts, knit rem sts, and cast on 4 sts. 8 sts. Rep from * until rick rack edging spans the 2 diagonal sides of the Shawl, allowing a little extra to ease around the point.

CLASSIC CARDIGAN

Designed by Kennita Tully

SIZES
Finished Chest Measurement

L	50" (127 cm)
1X	54" (137 cm)
2X	58" (147 cm)
3X	62" (157 cm)
4X	66" (168 cm)

Finished Length

L	29" (73.5 cm)
1X	30" (76 cm)
2X	31" (78.75 cm)
3X	32" (81.25 cm)
4X	33" (83.75 cm)

 ■■□□ **EASY**

Size Note: Instructions are written for Large size, with sizes 1X, 2X, 3X, and 4X in braces [ ]. Instructions will be easier to read if you circle all the numbers pertaining to your size. If only one number is given, it applies to all sizes.

MATERIALS
- LION BRAND® Homespun® **BULKY 5**
  #315 Tudor 5 (5, 6, 7, 8) skeins
  or color of your choice
- Knitting needles size 10 (6 mm) or size needed for gauge.
- Knitting needle circular size 9 (5.5 mm) for trim.
- Five 1" (25 mm) buttons
- Large-eyed, blunt needle

GAUGE: 12 sts and 18.5 rows = 4" (10 cm) in St st (k on RS, p on WS) on larger needles.

BACK

Beg at the lower edge with smaller needles, cast on 77 [83, 89, 95, 101] sts and work 1″ in Garter st (knit every row), ending with a WS row.

Next Row (RS): Change to larger needles and St st, working **dec for side shaping**: Dec 1 st each side on the 17th [17th, 17th, 19th, 19th] row, then every 18 [18, 18, 20, 20] rows 3 times more. 69 [75, 81, 87, 93] sts remain.

Work even until piece measures 17$\frac{1}{2}$ [18$\frac{1}{4}$, 19, 19$\frac{3}{4}$, 20$\frac{1}{2}$]″ from beg.

ARMHOLE SHAPING

Dec 1 st each armhole edge every row 4 [6, 12, 14, 12] times, then every other row 4 [4, 1, 2, 6] times. 53 [55, 55, 55, 57] sts remain.

Work even until armhole measures 10 [10$\frac{1}{4}$, 10$\frac{1}{2}$, 10$\frac{3}{4}$, 11]″.

SHOULDER SHAPING

Bind off 5 sts each shoulder edge 3 times. Bind off remaining 23 [25, 25, 25, 27] sts.

RIGHT FRONT

With smaller needles, cast on 37 [40, 43, 46, 49] sts, work 1″ in Garter st.

With larger needles, work in St st as for Back, working dec on left edge for side shaping. 33 [36, 39, 42, 45] sts.

Work armhole shaping as for Back. 25 [26, 26, 26, 27] sts.

When armhole measures approximately 8$\frac{1}{2}$ [8$\frac{3}{4}$, 9, 9$\frac{1}{4}$, 9$\frac{1}{2}$]″, shape neck.

Neck shaping: At neck edge, bind off 5 [5, 5, 5, 6] sts once, then dec 1 st every other row 5 [6, 6, 6, 6] times. 15 sts remain.

Work shoulder shaping to correspond to Back.

LEFT FRONT

Work as for Right Front, reversing shaping.

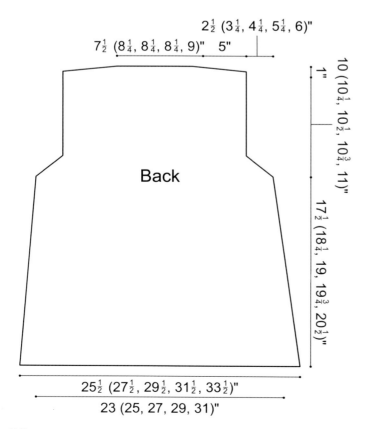

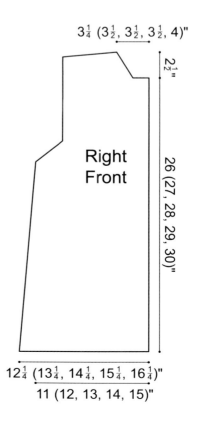